Painting the Heart Open

Liz Nakazawa

A Publication of The Poetry Box®

Editing & Book Design by Shawn Aveningo Sanders
Cover Design & Photograph by Robert R. Sanders

"The Missoula Flood" first appeared in *The Timberline Review* (Summer/Fall 2015)

ISBN: 978-1-948461-06-1
Printed in the United States of America.

Published by The Poetry Box®, 2018
Beaverton, Oregon
ThePoetryBox.com

For Vananh Nguyen and Malado Keita.
Thanks for all you two have taught me.

Contents

Painting
the Heart
Open

Searching for My Hands
in a Dream

Floating like a dream
knuckles lie fallow
bones hidden
beneath a lit up life line
heart line read quietly by the night
darkness and bloodline accepting
the finality of
morning murmuring of
fate line left empty.

The Painter With Her Back
to the World

the painter who has her back to the world
the world of bells, wings and sapphire
cottonwood and bones
tarantulas and tarantellas
a world of buckaroos putting up hay

this painter (palette nested beside her) faces the other way
the way away from the world
facing instead:
disappearing indigo paths and valleys
aquamarine bluff at vista's end
blue stories that boss us around
fears of both sleeping and waking
stories within stories
mournful endings and cheerful, yellow beginnings

her back to the world
she no longer commands her land
swiveling around instead to face
secrets of place, fugues and canons of personal history
whimsy, dream

    and those ships not out to sea

Four Rooms in Your Heart

don't keep only one open
pray to all of them

some corners could frighten
but there're also sculptures of ease

praise window and door
and the intimacy of enclosed spaces

bearing meridians
and the forgiveness of the rooms' divisions

equally laugh and cry
awake to the outside of seed and soil

don't keep only one open
pray to all of them

In Praise of Ink: Inside the Garden's Pavilion

I.

Abandon rain
and enter the show,
wa: harmony of ink and brush,
calligraphy of ecstasy and cloud
fish: swallowing heaven
persimmon ripe
prim crane.

II.

The master says, "Before I speak,
I'll show you what I do."
Pulls out a sheet of *hanshi*: smallest rice paper,
dips brush in black
quick strokes
adds water
ink thins
blots mountain
goat hair brush
dabs of pink and
bare plum bud appears.

III.

He smiles at a book,
hunts for the perfect Chinese poem
(one that Japanese know and love)
to pair with painting
something about flowers
not yet blooming.
Then he adds touches of turtle and sky.

Things to Believe In

clouds, all of them, including those on Cumulous Monday
   cirrus clouds and any that are comforting
      and the wisdom of lilies

delphinium, its blue good for borrowing anytime
   beets, color for dying pillowcases
      lyrics that never change

crickets in autumn, sheep
   dotted on thickly green hillsides
      trees that like to cluster

icicles (some are actually happy)
   windows that look over old barns
      gracious hay bales piled just for children and older dogs

Outside

On my walk
I gave up all ideas of evolution and atomic theory
regaling, instead, in sublime sauntering
devoid of the rococo
strawberries frantically growing to the left
cabbage in meditation to my right.

And who has not walked
in worthy moments
wandering
with a moniker of rambler
in unpredictable lengths of weather

becoming one of the fellows who goes it alone
a legato of striding
garrulous
excited
heedless
a little bit mad
semi-mechanical

thoughts folding into an origami crane

an allegory of emptiness
stitched to landscape, wind and sky?

Pendulous

the complicated anatomy of figs,
punctuation of acorns
and deeply moral
grapes, urging their own completion
of purple, reflect upon
what is substantial in autumn

nothing in this season
moves too far away from sun,
and the silliness of summer
reverts to careful

hours of days
shortening
toward upcoming icicles and frozen seed
relentless spiders interpret their craft
of innocence in amber light
and tall, definite grasses
hide poetry in their sheen

Before I Die

Before I die
I'll give you
a gesture of blessing
sudden bird
a story that can't be true
the shyness of violets
praise of jasmine scent.

I'll show you
the divinity of almonds
peek-a-boo of sunrise
the homecoming of hands
and saintliness of lemons.

Before I die
bring me a box
of your troubles
and I'll offer you
a velvet-wrapped ribboned balm.

A Drive to the Country

I left behind
the vernacular
the bone of my morning dream
and bellicose blossoms
sensing the upcoming
alchemy of a mauve afternoon
legible musings,

and on my drive
became a
message between city and countryside
wearing the joy of a carrier pigeon
carrying my pneuma
moving from the known to unknowing
stitching the city's convex,
to the country's concave

and drove through the gray
and splintered woods
every other cottonwood
sliced open from the shock of ice
this winter's breaking and
snatching limbs
in the thundering gorge
limbs like the empty arteries
of the dead.

I almost bowed to colors
that would come later
in that February sky
felt the clouds, orange
in my throat, on tongue, but then
the immediate spilled

[. . .]

yearning

and I succumbed

basalt cliff rose above
driving me to my knees to pray.

Doubles

I want to cheer up
a mourning dove
make a praxis interactive
silence thunder
goad a rock
place a blueberry in an estuary
limit lemons.

I want to chastise
a sudden cheetah
and double-cross
near the Crimea
dare a druid
dunk a darling
be partial to parallelograms

and do all the above
while in love.

The Day Before the Night

as light is captured
within the dark
you carried a candle on your dying lips
and miracles cocooned in the mundane
since this could be an ordinary act
my touch on your skin
the day before that holiness of night

like a familiar dream
dropped from the void
you slumbered
each breath taking longer to appear
then there were no archetypes
just your bones
stretched beyond sacrifice and obedience
and word retreating into shadow

the poetry of your brow,
blossoming toward some gentle
darkness at the back of the eye

Pray, As Earth Does

hold others steady
be a cradle for seed
absorb water slowly
help feed the hungry
manifest layer of rock
so young children
delight in its pebbles
hold others steady
crumble when needed
let others burrow in you
sharing their sorrows
hold others steady
be a friend to moles and badgers
hold others steady
offer a lap for horse chestnut, catalpa and fir
hold others steady
warm with the sun
pray: to hold others steady

From Tibet

From your wheelchair
you say you came to this country for freedom
after the Chinese bombed the
monasteries and monks of your dreams.
You offer me *momo*
your t-shirt boasting a yak: the animal
whose beads of bone are sold in China.
After some pleated moments between us
you wheel into your space of color
your prayer room circled by matchbook-sized
flags of blue and yellow.

Putting myself to bed later with the
smell of your gift of sandalwood incense,
woodsy with hints of vanilla,
I think of that tangled immigration
from your country of sky burial
where corpses were once wrapped in
white cloth and placed in homes' corners
for three days, then offered to mountains,
up to devouring vultures.

Yaks do best above 10,000 feet.
I pray in smoke that in our country
you'll have enough air.

The Face in the Sea

A town that lets the dead stay where they are
and agrees that the heart is simple:
it starts to tick and then it
stops.

A town full of folks,
like the fisherman,
one fisherman with a daughter
and the daughter remembered,
out in the waves,
a face in the sea, she said, out in the waves:
floating on the water, that water over fish,

fish over algae, algae over flagellum
flagellum beside hermissenda
the face in the storytelling sea, sea with veils of foam.

This town has few painters
and one wanted to paint that face in the sea
but the daughter objected to mimicry

and so, she said let the face stay
floating, philosophizing,
bobbing back and forth, like a maritime metronome,
quivering sometimes with pleasure,
alternating the novel and the familiar,
the melancholy and the blissful,
patient in an arpeggio of waves,
beckoning towards the silent
movie score: the shore

the face
watching over the town full of fisherman, the town which
understands,
agreeing, about hearts, harbors, ticking, nets and seas.

Golden

No suddenness in the sanctum
just your holiness full of thanks, jasmine and blessing
moss and fern give you outline
the sun places its light on your shoulders
allowing descending rays of grace to appear
quiet as water peppermint and orchis
sacred, yellow and happy

we turn to the autumn clock,
                    to the sharing hour

The Missoula Flood

I.

Deep in the Bitterroot Mountains
a finger from the Cordilleran ice sheet
moved south, through
the Purcell Trench
damned the Clark Fork River:
gave birth to Glacial Lake, Missoula.

Behind this plug
water rose and swelled
filling the valleys to the
east, the glacier buoyant,
and what wanted to be a river escaped
beneath the ice dam

draining the lake and
sending whorls of water to grind rocks
a race
through the Clark and Flathead Rivers,

picked apart bedrock
stripped topsoil
chiseled mazes
of buttes and canyons

Palouse soils scoured deep,
prow-shaped sculpturing
of gravel bars,
water-torn coulees and plug-pool basins.

In the Upper Coulee the churning river
yanked chunks of rock

[. . .]

from the face of the falls,
flooding collected in the Pasco Basin
pooled at Wallula Gap and then burst into the Columbia.

II.

Disaster, someone once said,
Is something wrong with the stars.

Was all this a
natural tumult, or a furious
rampage of our insecure earth,
a flood with very little reverence
and no misgivings,
impudent rogue waves lumbering
west to the Pacific?

Three days later it was all over, and
The beast was sung to sleep.

III.

The air was hollow and quiet, and
the silence, fecund,
presaging the generosities of
fifteen-thousand years later,
the flood's begetting:
the fertile valley's mint,
a vineyard snaking up a gorged cliff,
grapes of the loam's prime terroir,
and the swale of spring.

Sonata

the composer made a note
for the musicians to play this
slowly
as if in tears

an homage of melodic fragments
searching for their proper home
(the violin plunges into an
affair with the cello during the clarinet's lament)

but keeping chaos at
bay with a tightening theme
and variations haggling, properly enigmatic
right into bones of an emulsified conclusion

Tor House of Robinson Jeffers

At the cusp of land and sea in Carmel
we enter the dark cottage where
Robin and Una read Robert Louis Stevenson to the twins
(their small laundry flapping in the wind)
by candle, wrote and played chess,
the red horse and queen
now safely behind glass.

Rarely working in wood, only stone,
when he first began
building his home, one quiet stone following
stone, Santa Lucia granite, local rock,
rolled one at a time uphill from the beach,
bereft of a team of horses.

Then there were the mad additions: a top
stone from a pyramid of Giza,
salvaged slabs of a shipwreck's ballast
abalone from an Ohlone Indian
encampment on this land,
obsidian from Mt. Shasta,
slate from the Officer's Club at Fort Ord,
Portuguese tile, a gravestone nabbed

from a church in Ireland
that the Jeffers carried across
the country in their model-T.
Una said the stone turned her blood
to water and reminded her of
home in County Down.

Robin wrote poetry in the morning and worked
on the house most afternoons while Una collected

wildflower seeds from everywhere and Irish ballads.

All the books he loved are veiled
behind thin, gold diamond-shaped netting.
I squint to see titles as our guide
points to the 1911 Britannica,
the only book on display.

We're shown how the couple loved to
write on the wall in the den,
some Spenser on a dark high beam
a line from "The Faerie Queene" where the
Red Cross Knight pursues the good.

Into the bedroom we're led and are read
the poem about the death bed before us,
which Robin both hated and revered, and
the one he died in during the
unusual California snow,
the same snow that fell the day he was born.

I wasn't sure what phase the moon was in during
our tour but thought perhaps the tide had
receded a bit since the time
Una sewed white shirts with collars so her
husband would look more like a
poet and one daily hawk watched
Jeffers hew with stone.

Praise for *Painting the Heart Open*

"In poems of praise, memory, reverence for nature and the multi-hued nature of spirit, Liz Nakazawa's new collection captivates with 'secrets of place, fugues and canons of personal history.'

"Here, one finds 'sublime sauntering' or a 'legato of striding' from a poet who urges the reader in tender imperatives to 'enter,' 'abandon,' 'hold,' 'absorb.' Nakazawa's 'legible musings' range from the exquisite 'complicated anatomy of figs' to broad implications, geological and metaphorical, of the Missoula Flood.

"These poems, much like pages in a medieval book of hours, encourage the heart's light to shine while one is alive 'before that holiness of night.'"

~ Quinton Hallett, author of *Mrs. Schrödinger's Breast* and *Refuge from Flux*

About the Author

Liz Nakazawa is the editor of *Deer Drink the Moon: Poems of Oregon* (Ooligan Press), a collection of nature poems by 33 Oregon poets. It was designated as one of the Best 100 Books about Oregon in the last 100 Years by the Oregon State Librarian. It was also a Best Picks of Powell's. She also edited *The Knotted Bond: Oregon Poets Speak of Their Sisters* (Uttered Chaos Press), a collection of poems by 32 Oregon poets. Her own poems have appeared in *Turn*, *The Timberline Review* and *The Poeming Pigeon* journals and haiku has appeared in *ahundredgourds*.

She also has a background in feature article writing for magazines and newspapers. Her articles have appeared in *The Oregonian*, *Oregon Business Magazine*, and *The Christian Science Monitor*. She's also published in *Psychology Today*, *American Health and Fitness Magazine* and *Northwest Travel*. She has also taught freelance writing at Portland State University and at her home.

In her free time Liz enjoys bird watching, dancing (both folk and ballroom), calligraphy, reading, hiking and walking, identifying trees and flowers, writing snail mail letters to her son and friends, and collecting old books, vintage writing paper and stamps. She feels incredibly grateful for the love and nurturing, as well as friendships and community, from the pulsating Oregon poetry community. Words bloom easily here in Oregon.

You can connect with Liz via email: liznakazawa@gmail.com.

About The Poetry Box®

The Poetry Box® was founded in 2011 by Shawn Aveningo & Robert R. Sanders, who wholeheartedly believe that every day spent with the people you love, doing what you love, is a moment in life worth cherishing. Their boutique press celebrates the talents of their fellow artisans and writers through professional book design and publishing of individual collections, as well as their flagship literary journal, *The Poeming Pigeon*.

Feel free to visit the online bookstore (thePoetryBox.com), where you'll find more titles including:

Keeping It Weird: Poems & Stories of Portland, Oregon

The Way a Woman Knows by Carolyn Martin

Of Course, I'm a Feminist! edited by Ellen Goldberg

Giving Ground by Lynn M. Knapp

Broadfork Farm by Tricia Knoll

The Poeming Pigeon: A Literary Journal of Poetry
(each issue has a unique theme)

Psyche's Scroll by Karla Linn Merrifield

Impressions by Dr. Paul T.M. Jackson

In These Voices by Sherri Levine

and more . . .